Alive Again

Bible Study

Find Healing in Forgiveness

Sarah K. Howley

Alive Again Bible Study: Find Healing in Forgiveness

Flaming Dove Press
an imprint of
InspiritEncourage LLC
1520 Belle View Blvd #5081
Alexandria, VA 22307
www.inspiritencourage.com

To receive notices of Sarah's upcoming books, sign up at
https://www.inspiritencourage.com/book-readers-subscribe

Quantity sales. Special discounts are available on quantity purchases by churches, associations, and others. For details, contact the publisher at admin@inspiritencourage.com.

"'My son,' the father said, 'you are always with me, and everything I have is yours. But we had to celebrate and be glad, because this brother of yours was dead and is alive again; he was lost and is found.'"

Luke 15:31-32

Bible Study

TABLE OF CONTENTS

Teaching Videos Access

The Alive Again Teaching Videos are available exclusively online at the InspirtEncourage shop.

To rent the videos, navigate to https://www.inspiritencourage.com/shop/p/alive-again-video-bundle-individual-use-rental for details.

How to use this study

This study is designed for individual or small group study, with 8 sessions. It is designed to encourage thought and discussion of the scripture and forgiveness with no one 'right answer', but rather encourage individuals and groups seeking God to have discussions. For 'You will seek me and find me when you seek me with all your heart,' as Jeremiah 29:13 says.

General Guidelines for Individual Study

1.   Each session opens with prayer. Feel free to add your own petitions as well. Ask God to speak through his Word.

2.   *Alive Again* is the main text for the study, with each chapter and a few accompanying Bible passages and a video which support and expound on the ideas presented in each session.

3.   Read the Bible passage(s) more than once. Using different translations can offer expanded viewpoints on the meaning of the original text. This study uses the New International Version as the basis of questions and quotes. However, any version may be used to provide insight and assist in revealing meaning.

4.   This study is designed to guide you through forgiveness and healing for past hurts. There are questions in the book as well as this study book to aid in this journey. Writing your responses will provide clarity and focus your thoughts.

5.   Expect God to meet you in the study. His Word is living and active (Heb. 4:12) and he is present when we gather in his name (Matt. 18:20).

General Guidelines for Group Study

1.   Maintain confidentiality of the group. For participants to be willing to share and grow, the trust level in the group must be high. Do not share outside the group unless permission is given to do so. The nature of this study is personal. Participants are encouraged to share; however, it is also important to respect participant's decisions not to share. Each of us walk this journey in God's time, not necessarily in step with a group.

2.   Come to sessions prepared. Some groups will choose to read, view the video, and respond ahead of time then gather and discuss together; others will gather to read, watch, answer, then discuss together. Before beginning, agree how you would like to proceed so all are prepared.

3.   Be an active participant in the group by sharing your thoughts and responses to the questions. Groups often have members who are of varied maturity in Christ and each perspective should be valued. Remember to reflect Jesus' character when responding to what other's share.

4.   Listen to each other. Consider the amount of time that is available for all to share and be careful not to dominate the conversation.

5.   Be open. Be open to considering alternate viewpoints and agree to disagree.

SESSION 1

INTRODUCTION

Opening Prayer

Dear God, we thank you for the invitation to be transformed in your presence: heart, mind, and soul. Open our hearts and minds to your work in us. Be a lamp unto our feet and a light unto our path. We praise you and worship you. Amen.

Read

Luke 15:11-24

Alive Again Introduction

Introduction Video

Notes

Review & Discuss

1. Write out Luke 15:22-24.

2. List the father's actions from Luke 15:11-24. Note if the action shows Love (L), Forgiveness (F), and/or Reinstatement (R) and explain how.

Father's Action	L/F/R	Explain

3. Define prodigal in your own words. How have you seen God as prodigal?

4. The returned son is given three gifts in addition to the feast given in his honor. What might each of those gifts represent? Consider more than one answer.

Cloak	
Ring	
Sandals	
Fattened calf	

5. Picture yourself as the prodigal returning home to Father God. Describe how the imagery makes you feel.

6. Consider any squandering that you may have done over the years, like the prodigal. Is there anything that you may need to turn over to God? Turn it over now.

7. Take some time to consider your relationship with each person of God: Father, Son, and Holy Spirit. Consider intimacy, knowledge, comfort, and general relationship. Where would you like to deepen your relationship with each person of the Trinity?

Closing Prayer

Notes

SESSION 2

RECONCILED THROUGH FORGIVENESS

Opening Prayer

Father God, thank you for the gift of your Son, sent to reconcile us to you through the forgiveness of sins. The demonstration of your power through the resurrection glorifies you, your mercy, grace, and love. Prepare our hearts for your word and plan for each of us. Amen.

Read

Luke 15:25-32

Matthew 18:23-35

Alive Again Chapter 1

Chapter 1 Video

Notes

Review & Discuss

1. Write out Luke 15:31.

2. Compare the character of the two sons in Luke 15:11-32.

3. Which of the characteristics listed in the previous question might also apply to you? Is that pleasing or not? How do those characteristics impact your relationship with God and with others?

4. Describe the gift the man received in Matthew 18:23-35.

5. The amount the 'wicked servant' owed was 10,000 bags of gold. Scholars estimate that 10,000 talents are the wages a laborer could earn in *over 150,000 years*. What does this tell you of the king's character?

6. On page 12 of *Alive Again*, Sarah says that forgiveness is a choice. Describe why you agree or disagree.

7. Take time to complete the questions from the book, especially your definition of forgiveness, question 4.

Closing Prayer

Notes

SESSION 3

FORGIVENESS DEFINED

Opening Prayer

Dear Lord, send your Spirit today to fill us and guide us in your truth. Show us through your word who you are and what you want for us. Thank you for your word which is alive and active. Remind us of the price paid for our freedom and how to live free. In Jesus mighty name we pray, Amen.

Read

James 5:15-16

Alive Again Chapter 2

Chapter 2 Video

Notes

Review & Discuss

1. What is your reaction to the definition of forgiveness in Alive Again?

2. What might be reasonable barriers or delays to forgiveness? How can they be overcome?

3. Write Matthew 18:21-22.

4. Which other 'Bible words' do you associate with forgiveness? How are they related to forgiveness? (examples: enemy, reconciliation)

5. Share a time when you have struggled to forgive. What were the difficulties?

6. How did you feel about the forgiveness 'NOTs' (reconciliation, forgetting and excusing)?

Closing Prayer

Notes

SESSION 4

UNABLE OR UNWILLING TO FORGIVE

Opening Prayer

Dear God, thank you for your love that never fails. Thank you that you promise to never leave us nor forsake us. Strengthen us with your peace. Soften our hearts and focus our minds, that we may be your faithful servants. Amen.

Read

Genesis 16, Genesis 21:1-21

Alive Again Chapter 3

Chapter 3 Video

Notes

Review & Discuss

1. Chapter 3 considers three reasons that people struggle with forgiveness. How do the following verses support the idea that the listed reason can be overcome?

    a. Forgiveness earned: Ephesians 2:8-9, Luke 23:34, Ephesians 4:31-32

    b. Unforgiveness as Punishment to Others: Luke 7:47, Proverbs 17:9, Matthew 6:14-15

    c. Lack of Trust in God: Isaiah 40:28-31, Isaiah 55:11, Romans 8:28

2. Consider the character of God and list some of his attributes.

3. Which of God's attributes help firm up the foundation of your faith so you can fully trust him to take care of the offender and bring full healing to you? (Consider: good, just, unchanging, infinite, omnipotent, gracious, holy, sovereign, omniscient, wise, faithful, and more.) Choose 2-4 attributes and explain why they are key in trusting God.

4. God has already redeemed our pain; he went to the cross for our afflictions as much as for our sin (See Isaiah 53:4-5). However, when we are in the midst of the pain of an offense, we often feel that something has been taken from us or something was stolen.

In chapter 2 of the study book, you reflected on a time when forgiveness was difficult. Consider now if there was something in that situation that felt stolen or taken away as well. Share what you would like to see God restore.

Closing Prayer

Notes

SESSION 5

FLAGS OF HIDDEN HURT AND UNFORGIVENESS

Opening Prayer

Our Father, send your Spirit, that we may be filled with your Spirit not of fear, but of power, love, and self-control. Send your Spirit, full of wisdom and understanding to counsel us in your ways and in your truth. Reveal yourself to us through your word, your son, and our time with you in prayer. In Jesus name, Amen.

Read

Habakkuk 1:1-2:14

2 Samuel 11:1-12:25

Alive Again Chapter 4

Chapter 4 Video

Notes

Review & Discuss

1. On page 51, Sarah says 'This [healing] was not an overnight thing – this was an over time thing.' How do you respond to that?

2. Chapter 4 looks at flags that indicate we may have hidden unforgiveness in our lives. Consider Hagar and the wrongs committed against her from Genesis chapters 16 and 21; consider Sarai/Sarah as well.

    a. How do the women demonstrate inappropriate reactions, uncharacteristic behavior, or regret?

    b. How do the women try solving the problem themselves versus how God solves the problems and what benefits were in God's solution?

3. Another indicator we might notice when considering our own behavior, reactions, and feelings is our stress. Are there people who, when thinking about spending time with them, cause us stress? Ponder your relationship with this person to understand if there is unresolved forgiveness. Are there flags of unforgiveness there?

4. When Joseph was sold into slavery, Judah was the brother that had the idea (Genesis 37:26). It was also Judah in Genesis 43:8-9 who promises to be held responsible for Benjamin and speaks up to do just that (Genesis 44:30-34). These actions might reveal that Judah carried guilt for his past. Discuss if this guilt was also a regret, if he had a change of heart, and if he had forgiven himself. Include evidence to explain your answer.

5. God promises forgiveness for us in both the Old Testament and the New. Read Psalm 130:3-4 and 1 John 1:9. How do you respond to them? What stands out to you?

6. What hope do we have for our irrational or uncharacteristic responses?

7. Consider your actions and attitude in the past week. Have there been times where you have not responded as you should? Ask the Lord to reveal any underlying pain and to note any flags of unforgiveness.

8. Reflect on your feelings toward institutions or groups, especially those of the past. Do any flags of unforgiveness come forward in your mind? Jot down the wrongs that you have experienced from these groups. Follow that by praying for the group or institution and for forgiveness to bloom in your heart.

Closing Prayer

Notes

SESSION 6

I STILL HURT, I STILL REMEMBER

Opening Prayer

Abba, Father, we believe in you, we trust you. You are Yahweh-Rapha, Healer. Heal us and restore us through your word, your truth, your counsel. Show us how to fight our memories and live in your freedom. We praise you and give you all glory and honor. Amen.

Read

Mark 10:46-52

Matthew 9:2-8

2 Peter 1:3-8

Alive Again Chapter 5

Chapter 5 Video

Notes

Review & Discuss

1. Write out Jeremiah 30:17a.

2. What does Jeremiah 30:17 tell of God's thoughts toward you?

3. In the account of the healing of the paralytic in Matthew 9, Jesus first tells the man his sins are forgiven then he heals him. What does this tell us of Jesus' priorities for believers?

4. Which promises of God have carried you through difficult times in your life?

5. Which promises and truths of God speak most loudly to you in your healing from past hurts, especially those that have been your focus during the reading of this book?

6. In what ways could you interact with those who have hurt you to overcome consequences of sin instead of avoiding them? How could you show mercy and grace to those who hurt you or who you have hurt through the ripple effect?

Closing Prayer

Notes

SESSION 7

UNLIKELY RECONCILIATION

Opening Prayer

O Lord, we lift you up and praise you for your goodness and mercy. We praise you for the light you are in our lives and that your light and life shine forth from us. Give us wisdom as we live and work together. Show us the needs of those around us and give us the strength to serve those around us in our lives. Fill us with hope even in tough times and in difficult relationships. Bless our enemies. Thank you, Father. Amen.

Read

2 Timothy 4:14-18

Matthew 18:15-17

Romans 8:22-30

Alive Again Chapter 6

Chapter 6 Video

Notes

Review & Discuss

1. How do you feel about having "permission" to walk away from unrepentant and broken relationships? How do you think God feels about us walking away?

2. Sarah outlines five things that can be done to help us in broken relationships: Forgiveness Above All, Prayer Next, Wear the Armor of God, Love your Enemies, Hope in the Lord (pg. 81-85). Which of these do you anticipate being the easiest to implement, which the most difficult? What can you do to improve your preparation in the most difficult?

3. Read the prayer found in 1 Chronicles 4:10 and write it below, changing it into a blessing for someone you have forgiven and remain in broken relationship with. Make it personal to them.

4. Review the armor of God found in Ephesians 6:10-18. How can each piece of the armor help us in broken relationships?

Belt of truth

Breastplate of righteousness

Feet Shod with the Gospel

Shield of faith

Helmet of salvation

Sword of the Spirit

5. Think through the actions of Jesus when dealing with his enemies. Consider those who ridiculed him, whipped him, disrespected his father's house, and called him out for 'bad behavior'. How did he respond to these enemies in word, action, and attitude?

6. In consideration of the previous examples that you have noted on forgiveness in your own life, what are some concrete steps you can take to love your enemies?

7. Romans 8:24-25 speaks of hope. What hope have you placed in the Lord?

Closing Prayer

Notes

SESSION 8

BIBLICAL RECONCILIATION

Opening Prayer

Merciful Lord, give us the courage to live as Jesus did when he walked the earth. Show us how to open our hearts and release any residual bitterness and fear. Fill us with your love to overflow from our hearts. Send your Spirit to guide us in our relationships, that they may reflect your light into the world. You have overcome, praise to you! In Jesus' name, Amen.

Read

2 Corinthians 5:17-21

Genesis 33:1-17

Alive Again Chapter 7

Chapter 7 Video

Notes

Review & Discuss

1. Esau was terribly hurt by his brother Jacob, so much so that he swore to kill him. Read the message Jacob sent to Esau and Esau's reply, found in Genesis 32:3-7. Can you see any tests or change of heart?

2. You read Genesis 33:1-17 at the start of this chapter of the study. Can you identify any other change of heart or tests? What is the result of the exchange?

3. Joseph tested his brothers in order to verify that he could trust them again. How do you define trust?

4. Consider the relationship between Paul and Mark. We know from Acts 15:37-39 that Mark left Paul, but by 2 Timothy 4:11 they were reconciled. The men worked side-by-side in proclaiming the kingdom of God. We don't know how this reconciliation came about but put yourself in Paul's shoes. Mark abandoned you in Pamphylia. What would you like to see happen before being confident in trusting Mark again as a fellow worker of Christ? Map out a path or tests as if you were Paul.

5. Joseph tested his brothers up to 'life' by asking for his brother and including his brother's life in the tests to re-establish the relationship. Consider one of your own broken relationships.

   a. Up to what level do you want or need to reset your relationship?

   b. What might be a good first step to mend the broken trust in that relationship?

Closing Prayer

Notes

Did you enjoy this study?

Please consider leaving a review which increases visibility for book sand helps others find what they are looking for.

Free Bible Study

Download a free Bible study guide and access all of Sarah's free resource library at https://www.inspiritencourage.com/subscribe

About the Author

Sarah K. Howley is the founder of InspiritEncourage LLC and the author of Christian non-fiction books. She is an espresso lover, bookworm, and Jesus-follower who is passionate about discipling and encouraging others.

As a teacher, she has guided and encouraged students of all ages to do well and believe in themselves even more than she does. As a church volunteer, she encourages and teaches Christians to approach God who longs for intimacy with us. As an entrepreneur, she helps believers grow spiritually and equips them with biblical truth to live the abundant life Jesus offers.

She holds a Master of Education and is a trained Christian counselor under the Chiesa Apostolica in Italia. Sarah and her husband live in Asia, their fourth continent together, where he helps feed the needy and she tucks into her books and writing.

Other Books by the Author

Alive Again: Find Healing in Forgiveness

I Am: The Son Reveals the Father by Name

Thriving in the Wilderness: A Devotional Journal

FLAMING DOVE PRESS

Made in the USA
Columbia, SC
20 March 2023

14041436R00028